ISBN 978-0-483-66698-6
PIBN 10108723

For support please visit www.forgottenbooks.com

1

Common School Problems in Chicago

AN ADDRESS

AT A CITIZENS' MEETING UNDER AUSPICES

OF

THE EDUCATION COMMISSION

OF ONE HUNDRED

OF THE

CIVIC FEDERATION OF CHICAGO

AT HANDEL HALL

SATURDAY, DECEMBER 1, 1900

BY

PRESIDENT ANDREW S. DRAPER, LL.D.

OF THE

UNIVERSITY OF ILLINOIS

GAZETTE PRESS, CHAMPAIGN.

Common School Problems in Chicago

Mr. President and Ladies and Gentlemen:

For the invitation which brings me before the Citizens' Education Commission of the Civic Federation, and others who have a quick interest in whatever concerns this great, throbbing, cosmopolitan city, for the discussion of matters relating to her common schools, I first make known to you my sincere appreciation of your confidence and my grateful acknowledgments of your polite courtesy.

The trust is not one which is to be taken up lightly, We have not gathered for an evening's amusement. The questions we are to discuss bear heavily, not only upon the good name of this city, but upon the security and the happiness of millions of people for ages of time. The discussion is to be earnest, with much caution as to facts, with respectful regard for the experiences of other cities and for opinions of weight which have resulted from those experiences, and with as much straight and direct reasoning as we can bring to it. It is to be pursued with entire freedom. We are to say what we think. We are to care little about what may have been said in a spirit of irritation or pertinacity by any whose interests are special and personal. We are not to criticise flippantly. We are not to break down wantonly. We are to give credit where it is due. We are to be tolerant of differences. And through it all we are to try and reach some definite conclusions which will help to solidify the opinions of busy men and women who are much interested in the subject, who see that the questions involved have become technical, and who only wait to see clearly what they ought to do before they take up the things which will prevent any from disputing that the school system of Chicago is better than that of any large city in the world.

KNOWLEDGE OF THE CHICAGO SCHOOL SYSTEM

It is of course well known that my knowledge of the Chicago school system is not at first hand. Such information

3

as I have, has not been gained from the inside. If it had been, you might question whether my opinions were not biased. It has come to me as the knowledge which most of you possess has come to you,—through some acquaintance with the men and the women who have been bearing the burdens of the system, and, more than otherwise, through newspaper reports. But my point of view has not been the same as yours. For fifteen years I was a practicing lawyer, in a considerable city, with enough of political activity to entitle me to be reckoned with in a small way. So twenty-three years ago I was elected to the school board. I can recall that, at the age of twenty-nine, it seemed to me that I was elected to own the schools and to give directions about teaching to the superintendent and the teachers. More knowledge and more age cleared up the delusion. For the last fifteen years the tendencies of city school systems have been a fascinating study for me, and the organization and administration of schools has been my only business. For six years my position has been such as to cause every item of information touching the Chicago schools to catch my eye and engage my attention quickly; and it has been my custom to square that information with the principles which have become very well settled in the minds of very nearly all of the leading school men in the United States.

It is doubtless the fact that the Chicago school "system" is not really a single system but a combination of many systems, and that these have hereditary differences. There is certainly every reason to believe that there are here as fine buildings and as capable officers and teachers, as are to be found anywhere. It is not to be supposed that the members of the Board of Education have not carried heavy burdens, and, as a general proposition, carried them with genuine interest in the best good of the schools. Surely the wonderful growth of the city has presented to that board problems of unparalleled difficulty. Let us assume that no one has been viciously at fault. We are not here to try a case tonight. We are neither to establish nor to overthrow facts. Let us assume, what is doubtless the fact, that the system itself is not without faults but that it is more responsible for this than individuals are. It is a matter of common knowledge that some evil things have come upon the system. Some people have been allowed to enter it, in divers capacities, who should have been excluded. Unquestionably it has some tendencies which should be checked. Undeniably there is an atmosphere about it which needs to be changed. One who is at all informed upon school matters can hardly refuse to see this. Practicially all of the thinking people of the city know it. Nearly every platform and every pulpit announces it. Every leading newspaper reflects it. Chicago is not singular about this. Every large city has had or is having the same experience. Cleveland and New York and Buffalo have moved already. Philadelphia and Boston and Baltimore are trying to move. To do nothing is hazardous. If the tendencies are unfortunate, if the atmosphere is unpedagogic, if confusion is increasing, then the longer matters are allowed to go the greater will be the wrong and the more difficult will be the regeneration.

SCHOOL ADMINISTRATION NOT A PASTIME

We might as well realize at once that such a great city cannot have the best schools without being eternally upon its guard, without standing at all times ready to protect them and frequently to put forth heroic efforts in their behalf. Making the plan of organization for such a system is not work for novices. The administration of such a system is not a pastime. The schools cannot be worth maintaining and be used to distribute compliments to the ambitious, or left to the mercy of the spoilsmen. To be worth the having they must be charged with definite functions; their great property interests must be managed by men who have demonstrated their ability to manage property by managing some of their own successfully; they must be taught by men and women who love teaching, and who can teach; the honors and the emoluments of the system must go to the men and the women who earn them; there must be an organization which can withstand the assaults of selfishness in whatever guise, and there must be an administration which is imbued with the purposes of the people who maintain the system, and which is free to attain, in its own way, the high ends for which the schools exist. To have this there must be much intelligence, much civic courage, and an occasional moving together of the forces of righteousness without any reference to political, social, or religious distinctions.

THE GENERAL SITUATION IS ENCOURAGING

The general situation is encouraging for such a movement in behalf of the schools now. For thinking men and women who can appreciate the price the peoples of the earth have paid for self-government, for unselfish men and women who would help on the common brotherhood, for courageous men and women whose red blood is worthy of the fathers of freedom, there is something distinctly encouraging in the world events of recent months. It lies in the new conception of the fact that notwithstanding the conquests for liberty, notwithstanding the great charters and the growth of the common law, notwithstanding excellent written constitutions and the full and free power of legislation, notwithstanding the development of institutions, —notwithstanding all these, good government is not a priceless boon and an accomplished thing so much as it is a weighty and an always continuing responsibility. The distinct encouragement comes from the better and the wider appreciation of the facts that laws are idle except as they are executed by capable and honest men; that men of parts *are* in a very large sense their brothers' keepers; that we and our neighbors and our children are, and are to be, dependent upon the spirit which is breathed into, and the vigor which is put behind the administration of the laws of our civilization; that the forces of evil are uniformly subtle, always active, and that, as of yore, they can be repelled by nothing but conscientious, aggressive, and practical warfare. The stronger confidence lies in the new realization that civilization imposes burdens quite as large as the opportunities it confers; that the opportunities are in jeopardy except as the burdens are carried manfully;

and, more than all else, that the splendid spirit of the
Saxon race is seen to be making ready to execute the plans
of its continued progress with a clearer understanding of
the difficulties, and with the same energy and precision
which have heretofore made that great race the preëminent
force, the undisputed leader of that marvelous intellectual
and moral advance which has, gloriously, marked the
recent centuries of world history. All this lends special
confidence and enthusiasm to any civic movement which
may be started now.

THE AMERICAN EDUCATIONAL SYSTEM

Our American educational system is unique. The
intelligence of our people and the conditions in which
they have lived have given rise to it. The germ principles of what the fathers called the "common schools" came
from Holland with the Dutch. Their heroic and successful battles for liberty in the sixteenth century had produced,
first in the world, the common school. The English, in
settlement times, had no system of common schools. They
were content with universities and tributary fitting schools
which unlocked learning, not to the common brotherhood
but to the sons of noble birth. When these two peoples
came together and finally assimilated in the New World
their institutions assimilated also. Nationality, the progress of democracy, the extension of the suffrage, appre-
hensions of danger, new conceptions of the functions of
a self-governing society, and new estimates of the vital
principles of human progress, made elementary schools for
the common behoof, at common cost, and governed by
common authority, universal. In time secondary schools
in all of the cities and larger towns, and many colleges and
universities, were added to the common system. Aside
from the common school system there have been, and there
are now, academies, colleges, and universities, set up for
gain or established upon ecclesiastical or purely philan-
thropic foundations, many of them of the very highest
worth. These have a part, and those of worth a very welcome and important part, in our system of education. But

I apprehend that there will be no dissent in any quarter from the proposition that the blood and bone, the sum and substance, of our vast and flexible American system of education is found in our splendid system of common schools.

THE "COMMON SCHOOLS"

This system is universal, and it is universally cherished. It is not a local system. It is at the door of every home in the land. Since it has come to depend upon the taxing power, it is subject to the authority which may exercise the taxing power. But it is flexible and adaptable to all conditions of life. As a fact it is left to be shaped and managed by the separate communities as long as they are disposed to manage it well, and practically, that is in every case. It may maintain every grade from the kindergarten to the university. It may have such adornments as intelligence and wealth are, in accordance with law, disposed to give it. It has but one limitation,—it must be a *common* system : not common in the sense of being cheap and ordinary, but common in the sense that it is common to all and that all have common rights in it   There can be nothing in it repugnant to the principles upon which and for which our nation stands. It must be clean enough and efficient enough for the best. It must welcome the poor, the weak, and the unfortunate. It must be so shaped as not to exclude the rich any more than the poor. It must stand for common ends, for invigorating and fertilizing the mind, for disciplining the spirit, for warming the heart, and for the evolution of character after our racial and national ideals. It is not the mission of this system to redistribute wealth. It is not its business to support people but to teach people. It is not to be made the vehicle for carrying compliments to men and women of political ambitions or social aspirations. It is not to fall down before the corrugations which have formed in the brains of specialists unless they commend themselves to the common sense. It is not to yield to novelties : it is not to give over to passing whims. It is not to adopt theories until they have shown that they will pan out in practice. It is not to attempt to supply all the knowledge every mature and more or less educated person may think the world ought to have. It must expect to leave the larger part for men and women to dig out on their own account. It must forge the tools to dig with, but it must not be so weak as to forget that men must get their strength and their sense through the digging. In a word, it must adhere to principles which are commonly accepted. Surely it must advance. But it must advance upon roads which have been explored. Nothing is so hurtful to it as steps which must be retraced, or which involve it in uproar and turmoil. It is not to adopt new features unless they are well grounded upon fundamental truth and can be sustained by common consent. It would have been better if the name which the fathers gave the system had always adhered to it in common usage. It is vital to the power of the schools that they shall never cease to be in truth and in fact " the common schools."

DIFFICULTIES IN THE CITIES

It is to be said without hesitation that the noble and unique scheme of popular education conceived by the people of the United States has gone forward to magnificent proportions and to splendid results. No one could have believed half a century ago that it would be so universally so generously, so cheerfully supported ; that it would attain such magnificent proportions ; that it would exert such an influence upon our common life and so engage the common thought of the multitude. So marked have these things been, so strong is tradition and sentiment now, that no one will permit the fact that there are some strains upon the ship to lessen his regard for the noble vessel which has suffered strains and successfully ridden troubled seas before.

There *are* strains upon the ship. They are at vital parts. They are in high and conspicuous places. It is not to be disguised that serious difficulties stand in the way of adapting this system of common schools to the conditions of our largest cities. A system which has reasonably met every need in the country, and in the ordinary towns, is in

serious trouble in the largest cities. The trouble arises
from the difficulties in keeping the schools in touch with
all the people, and in sympathetic and helpful relations
with all the interests which must sustain them. We will
undertake to discuss these difficulties.

DIVERSE CONDITIONS OF LIFE IN CITIES

The widely different conditions of life in the great cities
are surely to be reckoned with in shaping the life of the
common schools. The mingling of the children of the rich
and the poor in schools exerts a wholesome and leveling
influence upon our community life which we cannot afford
to lose. The poor cannot afford to lose it, and if the rich
could only know it their children cannot afford to lose it
either. Leaving out of consideration the few who bathe
in lavender exclusively and live in no other than the artificial life of a pink tea, the well-to-do desire their children
to shuffle with the crowd for they know that contacts with
the crowd are imperative to the making of men and women.
There is little trouble so far as differences in the children
are concerned. There are neighborhoods in cities, and if
buildings are not unreasonably large the constituents of a
single building are not so unlike in circumstances and feelings as to interfere with the homogeneous life of the school.
A little toning up now and then, a little rational adjust-
ment here and there, which can easily be done by intelligent superintendents and teachers, will obviate real troubles
in this connection.

But there is hardly a city of size in America in which
good, sensible, cultivated families are not regretfully with-
drawing their children from the schools because all their
hopes are centered in those children, because their physical
life is imperilled in the close atmosphere of unhygienic
schoolrooms, and because they cannot submit them to
teachers who cannot teach in the modern acceptation of
the term, or whose influence is not culturing and ennobling.
And the school system cannot long inflict loss and disap-
pointment upon such families as these without bringing
upon itself the most serious hurt.

OVER-AMBITIOUS PLANS

The work of the schools has come to be complex beyond reason. It will have to be simplified or much of it must necessarily lack application to the diverse conditions of city life. The teachers are not and cannot be prepared for all they are expected to do, the children cannot assimilate it, and the homes are utterly confounded by it.

All this has come from the confusion in the educational world about standards and values. This confusion is not unnatural, and it is not to be regretted. It has been stirred up by the advance of democracy in the world. It is the legitimate product of the most intense specialization in research, and of the most widespread intellectual activity in human history. It is, for obvious reasons, more accentuated among the people of the Saxon race than among the less aggressive races, and, for reasons quite as obvious, the confusion is more confounded in the United States than among the more conservative English neighbors across our great lakes, or the older and still more lethargic English stock over the sea. Our traditions and our ambitions have brought into the field every project that human thought can devise and every fanciful scheme that the human imagination can suggest. The conditions have been such that one man behind a scheme of his own has had more power to advance it than a hundred men who knew it was worthless or impracticable would exert to hold it in check. But the time has come for doing what the athletic boys call " trying out."

In the " trying out " process public sentiment must in time be the judge. The process is certainly beyond this occasion and utterly and hopelessly beyond me. But the newspapers and the women's clubs are discussing it and perhaps we may not be held guilty of unpardonable temerity if we shy two or three suggestions into the field of observation. .

Is it not time to determine that we will attach greater value to the substantialities than to the novelties ? Do we not owe more to the patient, steady teacher who trains minds in the bedrock principles of human learning, than to the vivacious one who breaks into a conference or a newspaper with a brand new scheme ?

Is it the business of the common schools to turn out specialists? I trow not. It is the function of the schools to turn out men and women. It is a profound mistake, and a mistake which weighs most heavily against the interests which cause it, to allow the specialists to shape the work of the elementary and secondary schools to their particular purposes. Human experience proves abundantly that the men who have broken out the roads of human learning, and who have accomplished things of moment to mankind, were boys who struggled and endured, who were not nourished on a prescribed diet nor pressed into artificial forms, but who became arduous through necessity and who were balanced by the plain work they had to do. Out of such training genius has always come, and out of such work it will never cease to come.

Is there not too much bending of the curriculum of the schools to the demands of the colleges ? The greater number of pupils will not go to college. Those who do go will do their college work better when they get there if they have not been paralyzed with impossible tasks, and if they have formed the habit of doing things they *can* do before they go. The amount of work, or the particular kind of work, is by no means as important as the acquisition of the habit of work, the development of the power to work. It may very well be questioned whether the college and university are not exacting too much of the schools below. If the high school is to be maintained in every town, if it is to hold the interest and sympathy of all classes in the great cities, it may well be surmised that it will have to do less rather than more than it is now attempting to do. And if the demands of the universities for so much work are excessive are not their demands for exact measures of particular things unreasonable ?

In the advance sheets, just received, of the last report of the United States Bureau of Education, Commissioner Harris says : "The University of Illinois has made a new and noteworthy departare in introducing an elective system of entrance conditions, carefully worked out in all its details.   This Udiversity has practically said, 'Send us capable pupils, well trained, with minds well stored with something, and we will not inquire too closely what that something is.' "   I may add that I have considerable confidence that the Commissioner is justified in his commendation, and that that University is right.

An eminent French scholar and writer has recently published a book in which he does his people the great service of telling them, in very plain words, in what, and why, the Anglo-Saxons are superior to themselves.   One of the principal grounds which he finds is that the ambitions of the French boys are directed towards professional and official life, and that the work of the French schools is uniformly shaped so as to enable pupils to pass examinations which admit to the professions and to official positions; whereas, English boys are trained to do things and fitted to shift for themselves in difficulties and emergencies.   It is certainly better to do things, and through the doing of things to acquire the power to do larger things, than to investigate the idiosyncrasies of examiners and to cram up momentarily in order to run the gauntlet of an examination. Are we not in danger of drifting away from some of the very things which the Frenchman finds in our affairs to commend.   And are we not floating into some of the very things which he correctly says weaken and emasculate the French people?

The same writer animadverts upon the German educational system and insists that it is weakening because it prescribes just what every one shall do; because it is too official and rigid and allows no freedom; because it is substituting scholasticism and dilettanteism for sturdiness; and because it is destroying individualism and taking away the power of personal initiative through the overdoing of things by the Empire.   He says that the French have been told again and again that it was the German schools that defeated France at Sedan, and that she must take up the German ways if she would regain Alsace and Lorraine. He disputes all this, and even cites the German Emperor himself. He insists that Germany is not so strong as in 1871, and because of the overdoing by the Empire in prescribing what shall be studied and how it shall be taught in the schools. Again, he says English ways are superior because their children may study what they will and their teachers may teach with freedom.

In all this there is surely much for us to think of. It may be feared that our French writer does not realize how much the solidifying of our system of education at great centers of population is eliminating the things he finds of most value in our educational ways. It may well be doubted if we ourselves realize the extent to which our ambitious educational designs are centering work upon hard and fast lines in the elementary schools, and upon lines which have never been productive of the ruggedest and strongest men.

It is true that there is another side to these important subjects, but it is also true that this is the side which must commend itself to the masses, and·which should appeal with most force to their representatives who are charged with the management of the common schools.

There is undoubtedly a very widespread feeling throughout the land that the work of the elementary schools has grown unreasonably complex and confusing ; that it is being subordinated to some interests or theories which are not of general concern. It is not certain that this feeling is not well grounded. Nor is it certain that the tendencies of recent years are wholly wrong. The fact probably is that the trend of events is good enough, but is being carried to an unreasonable extreme. Old Doctor Leonard Bacon used to say at Yale that "Some people must squeeze a good thing till it has to squeal." We will do well if we try to lessen rather than add to the things the schools have been set to do. We will do well if we remember that the flexibility of the American educational system is its chief strength, and if we endeavor to adapt the work of individual schools to their constituencies. We will do well if we do not forget that most children are going to earn their living, and gain their happiness with their hands if they do it at all, and that we will be giving strength to the country by so much as we dignify labor and enhance the common interest in the agricultural and mechanical industries. We will be worldly-wise if we set value upon a love for work and upon the power to work, and if we receive into the higher schools pupils who have shown that they can do something without so much reference to what it is. This is assuredly so as to the secondary schools, and it is measurably so as to the colleges and universities.

THE TEACHING

But let us pass on to the matter of teaching. Every parent in this city is entitled to have his child taught just as well as the city can procure it to be done. There are marked differences in teaching. The differences have been growing greater in recent years because teaching has come to be a science. Every well qualified teacher has made a scientific study of mental states and processes, and of the history and philosophy of mental development. Every well qualified teacher has studied broadly enough to possess more than the field he occupies, and to gain the poise, the culture, and the versatility produced by studiousness. Every well qualified teacher is a student still. Such teachers can be secured. Such teachers have been secured in overwhelming numbers in this city. It is the right of every parent to have his child in the hands of such a teacher. If it is not, it is his right to have a place where he can make complaint, and it is not merely his right but it is the business of the whole city to know that his complaint will not be lightly regarded ; that it will not be trifled with between one office and another ; that it will be seriously regarded ; and that justice will be done.

. This city has vast and innumerable public interests. It has none of more vital concern than this, that every true teacher in its schools shall be protected against "the world, the flesh, and the devil," if need be, and that the right of every parent to have his child in the hands of such a teacher shall be inviolable.

The right to good teaching on one side of a city is not

greater than it is on the other. It is not the function of a city to get some good teaching, or to secure good teaching in favored districts. It is the business of the city to prevent all bad teaching. If the teaching is what it well may be it will be good enough for any, and therefore good enough for all.

The teaching in the schools of a city is to do something more than solve problems in mathematics and construct sentences so that they will parse. It is to give character to the people, and trend to the life of the city. It is to breathe the spirit of unselfishness. It is to make the schools a moral force. It is to inspire pupils. Teaching that does not lift the soul is of little worth. The fruitfulness of teaching depends upon the interest of the pupil. The interest of the pupil depends upon the adaptation of the subject and the spirit of the teacher. Mental activity is quickened through the warming of the heart. The spirit of the teacher is to warm the heart of the pupil. Then the language and the science will go along all right and, what is better, gentle, steadfast, heroic, clear-headed character will be forming which will throw its warm glow upon the pathway of the teacher when the shadows grow long, and which will bring security and joy and fame to the life of the city.

There can be no such teaching as this unless it is *free*. If one is to be admitted to the teaching service who is deficient in preparation, or who lacks the spirit of the teacher, and it is hoped to keep her from doing harm through rules and regulations, through nagging by principals and supervisors and superintendents, the hope will hardly be realized, and confident and aggressive teaching will be altogether impossible. So long as teachers allow themselves to be confused by many books, overwhelmed by a multiplicity of theories, and paralyzed by innumerable directions, the teaching will be turgid. Teaching must be self-reliant. This city wants freeborn and unbound men and women in charge of its schools. It does not want insipid teaching. It wants virile teaching. Teaching to be virile must be free.

Organizations of teachers looking to the control of a

city school system, through political or other influences, are incompatible with the work of the teacher. There is but one ground upon which they can be justified, the ground of revolution. If teachers would not have politics dominating a school system they must not play politics or appeal to politics to gain their own ends. If a system becomes hopelessly vicious the teachers may be justified in revolutionary measures. Movements to regulate the taxing machinery of the city are foreign to the functions of the teacher. They may find temporary justification in the inability or the failure of the city to provide for the proper support of the schools. But, except on the rarest occasions, and for abundant provocation, they are not calculated to advance the force in the sentiment of the city. The thinking people of a city want the teachers to teach. They do not want teachers to dissipate their strength in movements foreign to their functions. They do not want teachers to have to take up matters which properly and lawfully should fall upon others. Again, they do not want teachers agitating in organizations whose poorly disguised purpose is to protect some of their numbers who cannot teach. As a general rule teachers will find it better to adhere closely to their teaching, to share in movements for the improvement of the teachers and the bettering of teaching, and to avoid associations which are not within the scope of this principle. It is better for teachers to appeal to a city than to attempt to control it. Employees who attempt to control, stir antagonism. No one likes to say things against what the teachers do, but disapproval of such movements as these can hardly be disguised. Employees who attempt to manage matters which they are not set to manage will ordinarily be left to their own resources. The teacher will stand on a higher plane who teaches well, who puts her whole self into teaching, and who, if misused, appeals in dignity and confidence for the justice which all the sane world would accord to such a teacher.

Every teacher in this city is dependent upon every other. In the common sentiment of the city the force moves on together. No one has such deep interest in all that concerns the force as the self-respecting and capable members of it. If unworthy influences prevail it will be the unworthy who get the benefit of them. One unworthy or misguided member, under a corrupt or nerveless government, may easily do more to tear down than a score can do, by strenuous effort, to build up. In such a city as this the work of all the teachers is interdependent and inseparable. Its excellence depends upon the plane upon which, and the directions in which, the thought and energy of the whole force move. Upon the harmony, cheerfulness, and enthusiasm of the whole body the quality of the work of the schools must depend. All teachers work for pay. In money they get little enough. Happily no true teacher works for money alone. Unless there is a continuous and a growing interest in the sound development of pupils, unless the investigation into the processes which produce sound development becomes more fascinating as time advances, unless accomplishment comes to reward the earnestness of effort and prove the correctness of plans and methods, unless there is compensation which cannot be measured in gold, the elements of the true teacher have not been present. But these happy conditions may be present under favoring circumstances, and they may be utterly destroyed by circumstances which antagonize them. The position of every teacher is not secure upon the basis of merit if she is not safe against unreasonable exactions; if she is forced into associations which are abhorrent; if the freedom of one must be bound in order to prevent another from becoming a disgrace ; if she must be dominated by innumerable officials with confused ideas and liberal salaries, and forced to fight, through fire and water, for the small stipend which is her right. Under such conditions as these there can be little true teaching, and the teaching body, as a whole, has small chance to advance in the esteem of the city.

THE SCHOOL BOARD.

The school business of the great cities has outgrown

the kind of government provided for its administration. The larger cities of Cuba, very small though they are, have more complete laws for the democratic and efficient government of their schools than the city of Chicago has. The reason is obvious enough. The Government of the United States has made those laws, made them all at one time, and based them upon the best thought and the latest experiences of the world. The laws which govern the schools of our own great cities are behind the conditions which have developed, and we do not agree upon modifications which the new conditions imperatively demand. With inadequate provision for school government the difficulties which are most serious in the great cities, and which we have been discussing, have served, in some degree at least, to remove the schools from the common use of the people.

Nothing so annoys intelligent fathers and educated mothers as to find that their children cannot attend school and keep well because of unhygienic conditions in the schoolroom; that their children are not taught as well as they know they should be; and that, notwithstanding popular government, they have no redress and no alternative but to send their children to private schools and pay twice over for their education. This is becoming very general, · and it is the peril of the common schools in the leading American cities.

Of course, under these circumstances, the complaints are many, and they are all laid down at the door of the school board. It is not to be disguised that there has been much neglect at crucial points, and much abuse of power by school boards. One member is reported as saying that he "could withstand anything but temptation." It must be admitted that the temptations are almost too great for human nature. The constant care of scores of millions of dollars worth of real property, the disbursements of millions in ordinary expenditures each year, the appointments to innumerable offices and to a force of many thousands of teachers, without located and individual responsidility, certainly creates temptations which would be beyond the resisting power of most of us. The troubles are the very natural products of unprecedented growth and of inadequate legal provision for government.

The schools of a city are part and parcel of a state system of education. The legislature passes laws for the government of the system. All it has heretofore done for the administration of the schools of a city of millions of people, with thousands of teachers, where the individual citizen counts for little and it is impossible to learn about details, has been little if anything more than it has done in the cases of towns of a few thousand people and a few scores of teachers, where every one knows all about everything that happens. It provides for a commission and delegates to it practically unlimited powers.

The commission is constituted sometimes in one way and sometimes in another, but in naming its members the initiative is almost always with one or the other of the leading political organizations, and members enter upon service with feelings of obligation to the political organization which has been instrumental in giving them position. Even if the appointment lies with a public officer and he oversteps party lines occasionally, it is too commonly the fact that this feeling of obligation is not lessened. This is, in itself, corrupting. The common schools cannot become an issue in our politics, and their administration has no more relation to party beliefs and party organizations than to the administration of the banks or to the running of an ocean liner.

But this is not all, nor is it the worst. The worst comes from unlimited powers and personal ambitions; from the multitude of details and the lack of individual accountability; from personal and social and club and church influence, quite as much as from political influence; from the very natural desire to please one's friends and be thought able to accomplish things; from the fact that there is little in law and little in fact to check all this, and from a refusal to see, or to admit to one's self, what harm it does.

We will pass by the results of all this so far as it bears upon the care of property, the selection of sites, the erection of new buildings, and the mere expenditures of moneys, by saying that in half a dozen American cities the school boards, without any division and centralization of responsibility, have the care of more property and carry heavier financial burdens than fall upon the governments in half of the American states, with executive, legislative, and judicial departments, working together and balancing each other. And one must know that this great business burden can only be sustained adequately and permanently by the most complete legal organization which experience has devised.

THE SCHOOL BOARD AND THE INSTRUCTION

But our chief concern must be with the instruction. The main purpose of the schools is instruction. The curriculum is involved; the teaching is technical. The only way in which competent and life-giving teaching can be secured and in which mere mummery can be avoided, is through training carefully in the high schools, and if possible in the universities; through normal or professional preparation; through closing the doors against all who are not adequately prepared, or who have not elsewhere proved themselves to be expert teachers; through suitable payment for expert service, whether in the first grade, or the sixth, or the twelfth; through purging the force of members who prove unworthy, or who show that they cannot teach; through security of tenure, and security of promotion on the basis of merit; through allowing people who can teach the opportunity to teach with freedom; through fostering a professional atmosphere; and through energizing the whole organization with the elixir of pedagogical life.

Regardless of what may be professed by the authorities every teacher in the system knows by intuition whether or not these things are being honestly done, and whether the purpose to do them is feigned or genuine. If these principles are observed in good conscience the teaching body becomes buoyant with life, heads are carried higher, self-respect grows, the work drives out distempers and tribulations, the teaching gives energy to the pupils and sends interest and enthusiasm into the homes of the city; if they are ignored or repudiated the force will be sullen and self-seeking and subtle, the teaching will be woodeny, and the schools will be regarded with indifference by the people.

Here is where the great strain comes upon the ship. Boards of education do not support these principles completely. If not completely, then not at all. The system is not safe against the flood if a single dyke is open. If the integrity of the power which appoints and promotes teachers is punctured at a single point it is hopelessly destroyed. Then it is not long before everybody knows it.

The school superintendent is an officer indigenous to American soil. In Europe the state minister of education regulates everything done in the schools. With our democratic ideas this is, as it ought to be, impossible. Our system must be flexible and adaptable. So the management of the instruction in sub-divisions of our territory falls upon an officer who has developed naturally out of existing conditions, and who is called the superintendent of schools, or more appropriately, in large cities, the superintendent of instruction. As a science of education has been evolved, the duties of this officer have increased in importance and significance. He has come to be the representative of the intelligence of the people in assuring scientific instruction, and hence in the preparation, and appointment, and assignment of teachers.

Unhappily, practices have not yet become fully established, and the superintendent is not yet, in most cases, surrounded by protective legislation. The place which he occupies makes him subject to assault. The assault is ordinarily in secret. We have now got to the point where no board of education appoints teachers without observing the forms of decency. But we have not passed the point where many members of such boards expect superintendents quietly to arrange the machinery so as to aid favorites. Nothing so angers one in official position as to have his desires thwarted by one whom he looks upon as a subordinate.

If the official's niece, or the niece of his friend, cannot be appointed, or being in place cannot be retained, the superintendent will never be forgiven. The superintendent will feel the effects of this secret enmity at frequent intervals so long as both remain in their positions. If the time comes when a superintendent has thus incurred the opposition of a majority of the board, he does well to call in the the newspaper men, tell them all about it, and abide the issue. If he has been consistently right the public will probably sustain him. If not, some other public certainly will. In either case he will carry the flag of common decency into the ranks of the enemies of our civilization, and, going or staying, he will have the very agreeable company of his own self-respect.

SCHOOL AFFAIRS IN BOSTON

The issue between influence and pedagogy in the schools is up in every considerable city in the country. In Boston matters have gone to such a pass that President Eliot recently said at a public dinner: "The greatest peril now threatening the public schools is the school committee (board)." Last summer that board refused to re-elect the superintendent and two supervisors. The trouble was wholly one of appointments. The superintendent (Dr. Seaver) has long been in the service of the Boston schools and is a most capable and conservative New England schoolmaster. Mr. Martin, one of the supervisors, is also a thoroughly trained and experienced New England schoolmaster. He has written the latest and best history of the Massachusetts school system. I think his claims are somewhat large, but no larger than must be expected of a Massachusetts man upon a Massachusetts matter. Miss Arnold, the other supervisor, was called from Minneapolis to the service of the Boston schools at a larger salary than had been paid to any woman teacher in the land because she was among the very foremost supervisors of primary work in America. There was nothing to be said against any one of the officers personally. They were "held up" for months and then re-elected, discredited before tens of thousands of school children, humiliated before thousands of teachers whom it is their duty to supervise, by the small politicians both republicans and democrats, because they persisted in carrying out a proper rule concerning appointments which the board itself had made.

In June, 1898, after an all-night session, the board adopted what are known as "the new rules," one of which gave the superintendent power to appoint all teachers subject to the approval of the board. This rule was put in operation. At the next election the political organizations were active, and the members of the board who had stood for reform, and who came up for re-election, were beaten. Things went on in this way until the small fry politicians were in possession of the board. Not daring to breast public sentiment and repeal the rule, they undertook to " sand bag " the superintendent in the dark. He would not surrender. The circumstances were such as is commonly the case. He could say little or nothing. Unable to contain their rage the members of the board refused, in June last, to re-elect him and his two principal advisors. The public was aroused. Every newspaper in Boston, save one, voiced the common indignation. In confusion, the board re-elected the officials. But think how all this wears upon men and women, and what humiliation and confusion it brings upon the educational system of a great city.

THE CLEVELAND CASE.

The city of Cleveland has almost uniformly had excellent schools. The people have been very jealous of everything which interfered with their efficiency. Freese, Rickoff, and Hinsdale, names familiar to American educationists, were strong superintendents. For many years they held the initiative in the appointment of teachers, and a strong force of most uniform excellence resulted. Euclid avenue and the iron-works district both patronized the schools. In 1892, however, the city woke up to the fact that a less positive superintendent, though a good teacher and an excellent man, had been overrun by the spoilsmen, and that a considerable number of dark-lantern appointments had been made. Four leading citizens, not connected with the schools, framed a bill upon principles which they thought would give the city a sound school administration. It created a board of education consisting of a school director and a council of seven members, all to be chosen at the municipal election, the director to hold for two years, and the members of the council for three years each. The council is the legislative power in the system. It .can make no appointments. It only passes resolutions which must be entered in full upon its journal. The director is the chief executive officer of the system. He sits in the council with the right of discussion, but not of vote. He may veto acts of the council. He is charged with the care of property. He appoints and removes janitors. All contracts are made in his name, and he is responsible for their execution. He has unrestricted executive control of all business matters of the whole school system, and must answer for them individually.

The integrity of the teaching force was sought to be made safe by creating a superintendent of instruction, with legal prerogatives. He was given the unrestricted power to appoint, assign, and remove all teachers. The superintendent is nominated by the director and confirmed by the the council. His tenure is, as the law says, " During good behavior ;" but " The director may, at any time, for sufficient cause, remove him ; but the order for such removal shall be in writing, specifying the cause therefor, and shall be entered upon the records of his office, and he shall forthwith report the same to the council, together with his reasons therefor." This system has been in operation eight years. It has been of great advantage to the schools. It has withstood severe strains. The city believes in it. No one thinks of going back to the old plan.

When this law went into effect Mr. H. Q. Sargent was elected director and served eight years. His business sense was sound. He was steady and faithful. He never interfered with the superintendent. Everybody of substance was satisfied. But there were others who wanted the place, and some began to say that it ought to be " passed around " At the party primary last spring many neglected to vote and all were surprised when another was nominated.

Six years ago Director Sargent had occasion to find a new superintendent of instruction. He inquired closely for the best man in the country, and found him in Mr. Lewis H. Jones, superintendent of schools of Indianapolis. Mr. Jones is known to every prominent school man in America as a quiet man with much reserve, a kindly man who never harmed another, and yet a man with a square under jaw which refuses to allow any man to run over him. There is no deeper student of pedagogy, and no more experienced or more respected superintendent in the land. He did not seek appointment at Cleveland, but he accepted it, and has since gone quietly and satisfactorily on his way to the betterment of the schools.

As the campaign warmed up, the people, very anxious to support a capable man whom they believed to be conscientiously trying to do his duty, inquired of Candidate Bell if he had any designs against Superintendent Jones. The inquiry was pressed so hard that he had to say something, and finally published the following letter dated on the 19th of last March.

To the Citizens of Cleveland:

"In view of the fact that false reports have been circulated throughout the city to the effect that it has been my intention, if elected to the office of School Director, to interfere with the educational department of our public schools by removing the present superintendent, Mr. Jones, and many principals and teachers, I deem it but just to the public to make an open declaration regarding such reports. I have never at any time entertained an intention to remove either Mr. Jones or any other member of the educational staff, nor have I ever expressed such intention to any one, and any and all reports to the contrary are willfully false.

"My pre-primary campaign having been conducted without making a pledge or promise with reference to any position or appointment, I had hoped to continue up to the election free from all such pledges or promises; but knowing how sacred a regard the people of this city have for our educational system, and how jealously they would resent any material interference of the above reports, I have concluded to forego my original desire of making no pledges or promises, and say finally to the people of Cleveland that I shall not interfere with the educational department of our public schools, but shall leave that part of the work to the superintendent, where the spirit of the law, I believe, intends it shall be left.

"If elected to the office of Director, as I surely shall be, it shall be my constant aim to conduct the executive branch of the work in harmony with the educational branch; and *knowing the reputation and ability* of Superintendent Jones as an educator, I feel confident that, as Director, I could work in perfect harmony with him. "THOMAS H. BELL."

Having been elected, and some people being unspeakably hungry, he wrote the following letter of dismissal, framed under the law, to the superintendent on the 2d day of July :

"MR. L. H. JONES,
SIR:
     You are hereby removed from the position of superintendent of the schools of the city district of the city of Cleveland, and your employment by the Board of Education of said city school district as superintendent, is hereby terminated.
     I take this action because of incompetency, inefficiency, neglect of duty and misconduct. I believe that the best interests of the schools demand your removal and the appointment of a man possessing the necessary requirements.
THOMAS H. BELL, School Director."

But happily the law and the sentiment of the people proved too strong for such scandalous business as this. But for the law the superintendent would have been refused reëlection or badgered out of office without the necessity of assigning any reason. There was an immediate uproar, such as that director never heard before. Every newspaper, every pulpit, and every club denounced the perfidy. A well organized citizens' movement began legal proceedings to oust the director, under the public officers' act of the state ; but he threw up his hands, said he would stop if they would, and withdrew his letter to the superintendent. The people did not agree to his proposition. He desisted but they are going on.

But again I say, think of the wear and tear of all this upon superintendents and teachers, and of its malevolent influence upon the schools.

I have referred to this and to the Boston case, quite fully, to show how very deep-seated and pernicious are the influences which are opposed to the sound administration of the schools, and because so few people realize the fact.

THE " ONE-MAN " POWER.

There is no time now to go into any very full discussion of what some interested people have sought to make odious by calling it the "One-Man" power in school administration. But this may be quickly said. The functions of a school superintendent are executive, and executive functions cannot be effectually performed by more than one responsible man. The security of good teaching in a great city is dependent upon the centering of legal authority and accountability. We may work up to it by easy stages, but we will all get there after awhile. We may perhaps stop awhile with the right of initiative. When the board of education of this city confers *that* right by resolution, and directs the superintendent to report recommendations which are made to him touching nominations he makes, it shows that it understands the whole situation, and it logically concedes the whole case, so far as actual practice is concerned. I doubt if there is a member of the board who does not know very well that, to be effective and enduring, that right will have to be conferred by something stronger than a resolution of the board. No one interested in good teaching has ever proposed appointments by a superintendent except from an eligible list constituted according to law, and with ample assurances as to the publicity of every step of the process which results in appointment. Examinations are much better than nothing, but teaching is not merely a matter of knowledge, or of the ability to pass examinations. It is a matter of spirit, and of power, and of adaptability, and of application. The public is not long going to deprive itself of educational officials who can measure all those qualities correctly merely because individuals or organizations want to leave the way open to help their own regardless of all those things. Every one with any experience knows that no superintendent would ever remove a teacher, no matter how defective, unless self-responsibility made it imperative. And every one with any experience also knows that where the power of removal is lodged among several men, and they can shuffle the responsibility between them, no teacher, no matter how defective, will ever be removed. It is idle to discuss mere theories, either from a selfish, or from an academic standpoint. The people of our large cities are coming to know what good teaching is. They are going to have it for their children. The spirit of brotherhood is going to lead the strong and well-to-do to assure it to the children of the weak and the poor. And without regard to talk about "**One-Man**" power they are in time going to have matters so fixed, that if their children are in rooms where physical conditions cause frail life to languish, or if their children are in the hands of those who cannot teach, they can go down town and find the particular man who is charged with the legal obligation to correct the one wrong or the ,other, and expect, and if necessary require, him to do it. The so-called " One-Man" power is theoretically sound, and practically necessary. The superintendent is the instrument of the people to accomplish a particular thing. He is more responsive to the rights of the citizen than a board can possibly be. The best democracy I know of is that which enables democracy to accomplish its own ends and perpetuate itself.

CONCLUSION

Coming to a conclusion, which has been too long delayed, I submit a few propositions which are, to me at least, obvious.

1. Nothing should be done touching the elementary schools which is calculated to interfere with their being "common schools," that is of equal interest and advantage to all of the people.

2. The work of the schools should be made less, rather than more, complex; and less, rather than more, advanced work should be demanded in the grades. The standards of values should recognize the habit of work, and the love of it, quite as much as the amount of work performed.

3. Public secondary schools and advanced schools have abundant sanction in public policy. Their necessity to the steady and scientific advance of the elementary schools is imperative This of itself would be abundant ground to justify them if there were no other grounds. There are many other grounds. The whole question has passed beyond the phase of dispute. But the higher schools are bound to carefully refrain from changing the "common school" character of the lower schools.

4. The most subtle and deadly enemy of the schools is influence in the interests of persons, or parties, or sects,

which does not consider the common welfare of the whole mass. The school organization must be required to resist all such influences, and must be given the legal right and power to do it.

5. A board of education should be small in numbers, and its members should stand for the whole city, and not represent districts of it. In some way the temptation to talk to the galleries should be taken away. The members should be representative of the business and property interests, as well as of the intelligence and genuine unselfishness of the city.

6. The board should be vested with legislative power alone. It should have no appointments beyond the imperative necessities of the case. If vested with the appointment of a business manager and superintendent, these officers should be given long terms and statutory powers which will enable them to perform their functions without hindrance. Whatever the board does, should be required to be within the scope of its statutory functions, and by resolution to be entered upon its journal.

7. The school system and the municipal system should have no relations. And in the school system business matters and instructional matters should be completely separated. The instruction must be of first importance and saved harmless from everything else.

8. Executive action upon all business matters should be vested in a business manager. He should be given ample authority, and be afforded adequate help, to care for all business concerns. He should represent the board in all contracts, and see that they are completely and honestly executed. He should be charged with the care of all buildings, and to that end should appoint and remove superintendents, and janitors, who have immediate charge of them. If the board is cheated in its business, if buildings are unwholesome, he should be held accountable.

9. The instructional work should center in a superintendent of instruction. He should be charged with nothing but the courses of instruction and the quality of the teaching. His tenure should be long and fixed. His powers

should be clearly defined in the law, and within the scope of his responsibility they should be complete. He should appoint, assign, and for cause remove teachers. Teachers, other than such as have already taught successfully and acquired reputation, should be required to pass through, at least, prescribed courses of study in subject matter and in the science of teaching. Appointments should only be made from an eligible list constituted according to law; they should be made for a probationery period, and where continued after that should be permanent, with removal only for cause. Pay should be adequate for expert service, in whatever grade, and the scale should favor length of successful service, and the salary check should be as certain at stated periods as that of the governor of the commonwealth. Promotions should go to teachers who have the spirit of the teacher and can teach, who have steadiness and can build character, who demonstrate that they can carry responsibility. One who invokes influence should suffer for it. The highest premium should be put upon gentleness and culture, on strength of character and scientific teaching. The strength of the schools is in the teaching. The superintendent of instruction should have charge of all this. He should be amply protected, and given ample authority to meet his responsibilities. The right of every parent to the best possible teaching for his child should be supreme, and whenever this right is not made good the superintendent should be called sharply to account.

10. The law of the State should clearly define the machinery of the system and fix the powers of all connected with it. Statutory law might very well express in terms the aims and purposes of the people more than it does. The spirit is quite as important as the letter of the law. And the law should assure the fullest publicity about everything that is done in connection with the schools.